CALIFORNIA

The Wine Country Inn, St. Helena

COUNTRY INNS OF AMERICA

California

A GUIDE TO THE INNS OF CALIFORNIA

BY PETER ANDREWS AND GEORGE ALLEN

DESIGNED BY ROBERT REID

HOLT, RINEHART AND WINSTON, *New York*
THE KNAPP PRESS, *Los Angeles*

Frontispiece photograph
The pavilion at Avalon photographed
from the Zane Grey Pueblo Hotel
by George W. Gardner.

Copyright © 1980 by Knapp
Communications Corporation.
Published in the United States of
America in 1980.
The Knapp Press
5900 Wilshire Boulevard, Los
Angeles, California 90036.
All rights reserved, including the
right to reproduce this book or
portions thereof in any form.
Trade edition distributed by Holt,
Rinehart and Winston in the
United States and simultaneously
by Holt, Rinehart and Winston of
Canada, Limited.

Library of Congress Cataloging in Publication Data
Andrews, Peter, 1931–
    Country inns of America.

    Vol. 3 by P. Andrews and T. Ecclesine; vol. 4 by
P. Andrews and G. Allen.
    CONTENTS: [1] Upper New England.—[2] Lower New
England.—[3] New York and Mid-Atlantic.—[4] California.
    1. Hotels, taverns, etc.—California—Directories.
I. Allen, George, 1936–   joint author.
II. Ecclesine, Tracy, joint author.   III.   Reid, Robert,
1927–   IV. Title.
TX907.A662   647'.94'73   79-22906
ISBN 0 03 043726 1

First Edition

10 9 8 7 6 5 4 3 2 1

A Robert Reid-Wieser & Wieser production

Printed in U.S.A. by R. R. Donnelley & Sons

CONTENTS

Photographed by Lilo Raymond
**Photographed by George W. Gardner*

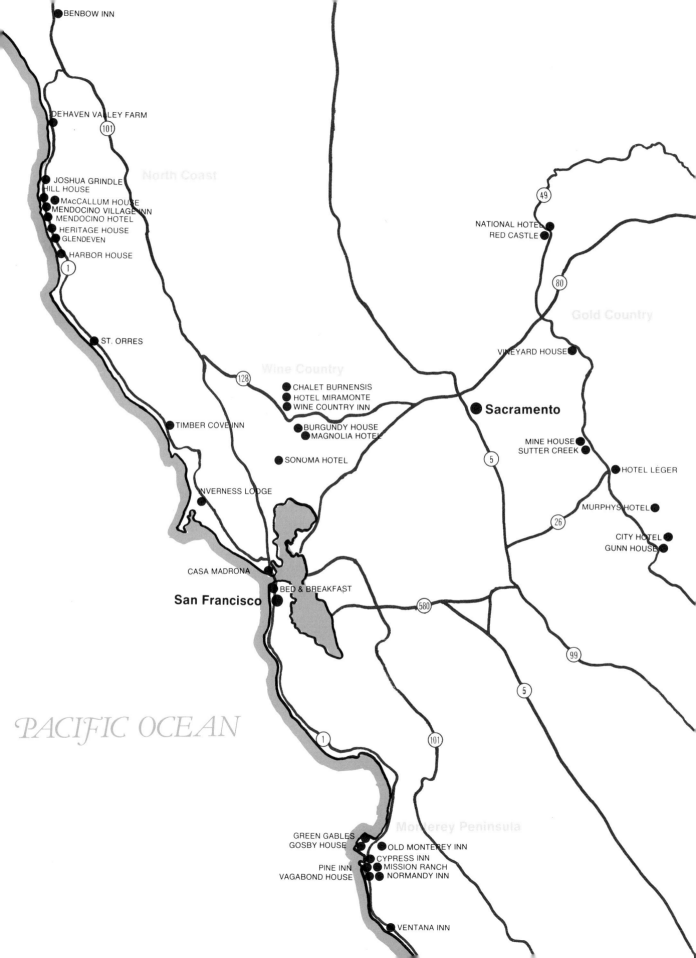

BENBOW INN

DEHAVEN VALLEY FARM

101

North Coast

JOSHUA GRINDLE
HILL HOUSE
MaCCALLUM HOUSE
MENDOCINO VILLAGE INN
MENDOCINO HOTEL
HERITAGE HOUSE
GLENDEVEN

HARBOR HOUSE

1

ST. ORRES

128

Wine Country

CHALET BURNENSIS
HOTEL MIRAMONTE
WINE COUNTRY INN

BURGUNDY HOUSE
MAGNOLIA HOTEL

SONOMA HOTEL

TIMBER COVE INN

INVERNESS LODGE

CASA MADRONA

BED & BREAKFAST

San Francisco

PACIFIC OCEAN

49

NATIONAL HOTEL
RED CASTLE

80

Gold Country

VINEYARD HOUSE

Sacramento

MINE HOUSE
SUTTER CREEK

HOTEL LEGER

5

MURPHYS HOTEL

26

CITY HOTEL
GUNN HOUSE

580

99

5

1

101

Monterey Peninsula

GREEN GABLES
GOSBY HOUSE

OLD MONTEREY INN
CYPRESS INN
MISSION RANCH

PINE INN
VAGABOND HOUSE

NORMANDY INN

VENTANA INN

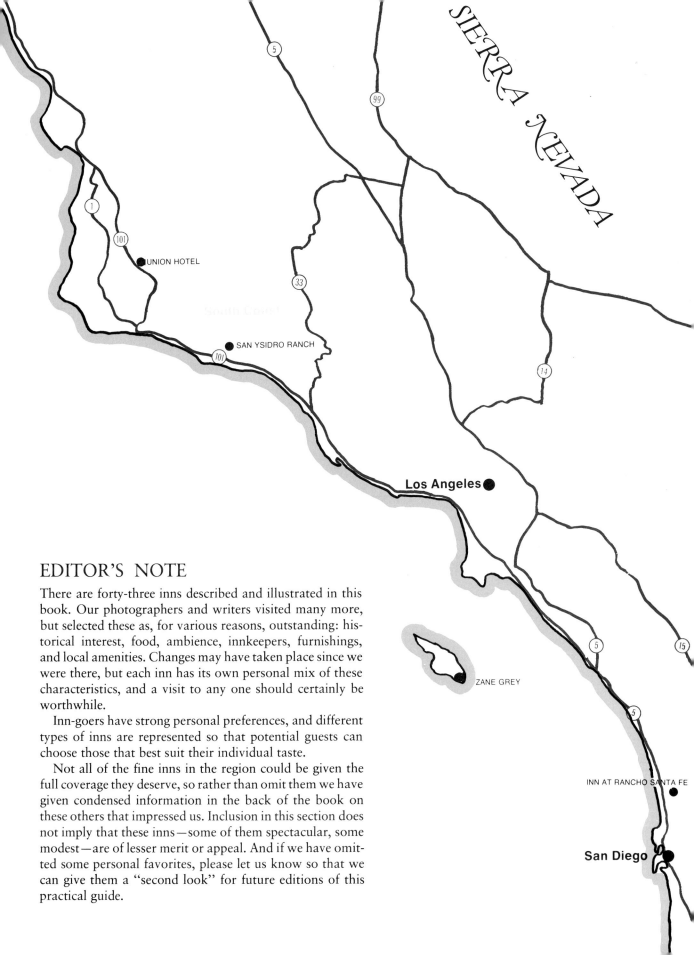

SIERRA NEVADA

5

99

1

101

● UNION HOTEL

33

● SAN YSIDRO RANCH

101

14

Los Angeles ●

5

15

● ZANE GREY

5

5

INN AT RANCHO SANTA FE
●

San Diego ●

EDITOR'S NOTE

There are forty-three inns described and illustrated in this book. Our photographers and writers visited many more, but selected these as, for various reasons, outstanding: historical interest, food, ambience, innkeepers, furnishings, and local amenities. Changes may have taken place since we were there, but each inn has its own personal mix of these characteristics, and a visit to any one should certainly be worthwhile.

Inn-goers have strong personal preferences, and different types of inns are represented so that potential guests can choose those that best suit their individual taste.

Not all of the fine inns in the region could be given the full coverage they deserve, so rather than omit them we have given condensed information in the back of the book on these others that impressed us. Inclusion in this section does not imply that these inns—some of them spectacular, some modest—are of lesser merit or appeal. And if we have omitted some personal favorites, please let us know so that we can give them a "second look" for future editions of this practical guide.

Inspired collaboration of man and nature

Glendeven is a dream of ordered beauty, a place where house, lawn and gardens have been brought together in a kind of passionate decorum. Jan deVries had known the house long before he bought it. He first visited it years ago, and he says that in some way he's tried to duplicate what he remembered of the Little River farm in every house he has owned. When he and his wife, Janet, found the original was for sale, they felt destined to buy it and take over its care.

GLENDEVEN is painted on the mailbox, and the six-bedroom house behind the redwood fence and cypress trees might well be a private home. In its unspoiled setting on the Mendocino coast, here is an inn for calm reflection, where even the curtains at a window or the placement of a chair contribute to the sense that one is free to pursue the occupations of a bygone time.

On the main floor, a guest room looks out on the beautiful red barn of the New England-style farm. A soft down comforter on the bed is a perfect covering on the cool coastal nights, and Janet has made one for every room. Upstairs, the room called King's Crest has rich wine-purple walls; the Gold Crest has its own balcony; Bay View is as good as its name; and Mendocino Wood has a wall of beautifully weathered barn siding. At the top of the house is The Garret, where two skylights give a feeling of luxurious privacy, and muted colors are accented with a touch of chintz.

For breakfast, Janet serves fruit breads, juices, steaming coffee and tea in earthenware pots; and for each guest, a boiled egg comes to the table in its own tiny basket artfully made from twigs.

Outside, a rare acacia blooms in a corner of the garden, and various species of eucalyptus provide shade and exude their pungent fragrance. Pampas grass and cypresses, gardenias and princess flowers, all have their place. The porch gives onto a terrace edged with bright yellow flowers, and there's much for guests to see and do nearby. Down the hill is the Van Damme State Park, and two miles north the town of Mendocino spreads out along the headlands. But on most days, a pleasant stroll through the adjacent fields, with their candle pines, calla lilies and flowering Scotch broom, is enough. People can easily fall in love with this part of the Pacific Coast, and Glendeven is a good place to begin.

GLENDEVEN, 8221 North Highway 1, Little River, Calif. 95456; (707) 937-0083; Jan and Janet deVries, Innkeepers. An idyllic 6-room guest house 2 miles south of Mendocino on the rugged north coast. Private baths and shared baths. Open all year. Rates, including Continental breakfast, $32 to $40, double. Single $5 less. No other meals served. Children accepted at discretion of innkeepers. No pets. No credit cards accepted. Hiking, nature walks in immediate vicinity and in nearby state park.

DIRECTIONS: Inn is on Route 1, north of Van Damme State Park, just 2 miles south of Mendocino and north of the small village of Little River.

Originally a farmhouse, now an outstanding country inn with a variety of sumptuous bedrooms.

Hollywood set piece on a rugged coast

Built on an oceanside landscape of high bluffs and steep coastal slopes, the village of Elk, on the rugged northern coast of California, seems as isolated and remote as it is beautiful. Elk had its beginning as a prosperous lumber camp, where dizzying trestles, connecting the mainland to the huge offshore rocks sculpted by the sea, were used to load lumber from the nearby Albion forests onto schooners bound for San Francisco.

In 1917, the Goodyear Lumber Company built Harbor House as a guest lodge for entertaining corporate executives and customers. A larger version of the redwood model house built for the Panama-Pacific International Exposition in 1915, it was a company showpiece. Built on a cliff, Harbor House faces Elk's most imposing seascape, a cove with craggy promontories and rocks tunneled by the sea that look like the inspiration for some of Henry Moore's sculptures.

Innkeeper Pat Corcoran administers Harbor House with a sure and somewhat autocratic hand. "For breakfast," she explains, "guests are likely to get whatever I'm in the mood to cook. I do serve substantial dinners. Good soups, then local fish or a chicken dish or some rather good stuffed pork chops and the freshest vegetables I can find. But I outdo myself with the desserts—I specialize in tortes." The food has to be good. It competes with a dining room panorama of the cove and a stunning view of every Pacific sunset.

The style at Harbor House is ruggedly casual. "The climb down the cliff to our private beach is not simply a nice civilized jaunt," says Pat, "so I can be pretty sure my guests aren't going to go bird-watching in white flannels."

The guest rooms in the main house have the atmosphere of Hollywood versions of executive retreats.

One upstairs room, in green and white, is half the length of a sound stage, with large beds, triple-mirrored vanities and chaises longues. Downstairs is an even larger wood-paneled room, really a suite, with a well-stocked library of books on nature, ecology and geology.

The vast redwood-paneled living room has an Edwardian flavor, with lots of good magazines, a piano and perhaps the world's largest collection of guitar records beside the stereo. Harbor House manages to be both formal and casual at the same time, a unique building in a stunning setting.

HARBOR HOUSE, 5600 South Highway 1, Elk, Calif. 95432; (707) 877-3203; Pat Corcoran, Innkeeper. A unique 5-room inn, with 4 cottages, on a high bluff above a spectacular ocean cove. Private baths. Fireplaces in most rooms, Franklin stoves in cottages. Open all year. Rates $65 to $85 double, including dinner and breakfast served to overnight guests only. Children not encouraged. Pets allowed in cottages. No credit cards accepted. Private beach in cove down a cliff path. Fishing and skin diving nearby.

DIRECTIONS: Inn is 17 miles south of Mendocino on Route 1, just north of the village of Elk, midway between Mendocino and Point Arena.

Expansiveness is the word to describe Harbor House, from the ocean view at left, to the cedar paneled lounge above, to the luxurious guest room overleaf.

Oceanside retreat to luxury

For such an elegant establishment, Heritage House has had an unusually racy past. It was built in 1877 by the grandfather of the present innkeeper for a lumberman who used the cove at the base of the cliffs as a shipping point for redwood ties. Over the years it came to have less honorable uses. Illegal aliens, primarily Asians who provided cheap labor for building the railroads in the late 1800s, were dropped off by the boatload; and during Prohibition, the cove was a virtual marina for rumrunners.

When Don Dennen and his wife were visiting the area in 1949, they found the house battered and abandoned but still boasting the graceful lines and fine craftsmanship of the "State of Maine" architecture so typical of northern California in Don's grandfather's time. The setting was spectacular. In an area where panoramic ocean views are commonplace, the house has an unmatched vista of cliffs, cove, rocks and ocean. Don recalls they made arrangements "within the hour" to buy the place, and he and his wife set about creating Heritage House.

The original house provided the nucleus, and other structures were added, with luxurious touches everywhere. The lounge, spacious and heavy-beamed, was originally an apple storage house, which they bought and reassembled after carting it twenty-four miles. It has a huge fireplace, comfortable easy chairs and round oak tables. The sun-dappled dining room, joining the lounge to the main house, has a window wall with views of the rocky cove below. The food consists of well-prepared American cooking, from the excellent soups and beautifully presented appetizers to the lovely dessert tortes and parfaits. The Saturday night buffet featuring prime ribs is deservedly popular, and the bite-size hotcakes from Mrs. Dennen's own recipe are a must at breakfast.

The limited number of guest rooms in the main building has been supplemented by cottages tucked away on the hillside. One unit has a sod roof, and all have been carefully placed on the landscaped grounds to provide an unobstructed view. Two of the spacious and luxurious newer units are La Maison 2, an elegant suite furnished with antiques, and the Water Tower, a duplex with a two-story living room and a balcony guests can sleep on.

Almost any country inn represents a retreat from the world outside. Usually it is a retreat to a simpler way of life, but at Heritage House it is a retreat to luxury.

OVERLEAF: Heritage House is a complex of simple buildings with luxurious interiors. *Top left and right*: a cottage called Stable, roofed with sod for coolness, and other cottages, overlooking the sea. *Below*: the extensive grounds have many attractions of their own.

HERITAGE HOUSE, 5200 Highway 1, Little River, Calif. 95456; (707) 937-5885; L. D. Dennen, Innkeeper. A luxurious 52-room inn on the north coast of Calif. Private baths. Open Feb. through Nov. Rates $49 to $77 single; $64 to $92 double; 2-room suites $82 to $105. Additional guest in room $25. Rates include dinner and breakfast. Dining room open to the public by reservation. Children welcome; no pets. No credit cards accepted. Tennis and golf available nearby.

DIRECTIONS: Inn is on Route 1 in Little River, 5 miles north of intersection of Routes 128 and 1.

Up-to-date Victorian on the North Coast

The idea that Victorians and the houses they lived in were somehow quaint is a modern misreading of that extraordinary period of history. The Victorians, quite properly, saw themselves as the most modern of people who built their homes with an eye for solid comfort and with appreciation of all the modern conveniences of the time, whether it be kitchen gadgetry, labor-saving devices or indoor plumbing.

The Hill House, set in the picturesque town of Mendocino on the northern California coast, is perfectly in keeping with its Victorian appearance. Built only last year, Hill House captures the spaciousness of Victorian architecture while providing each of the twenty-one guest rooms with its own telephone and private bath. There is also a color television set in each room, but each has been enclosed in a Victorian cabinet, discreetly hidden from those who prefer looking at the Pacific Ocean to watching reruns of "Gilligan's Island."

All the conveniences may be strictly up to date, but the accommodations and the service reflect the style of a century ago. Each room features either a king-size brass bed or two double beds and is furnished with a Victorian-style rocker, a large gold-framed mirror, oak tables and chairs, marble-topped end tables, hurricane lamps and an abundance of freshly cut flowers from the Hill House garden. The Fireplace Suite is much in demand, with its cozy seating area in front of the fire.

The Hill House will shortly be opening its own restaurant and bar, but for the moment guests are more than satisfied with a delightful Continental breakfast that includes coffee and homemade cake served on a tray and brought to their rooms.

The Hill House is situated in some of the most picturesque country on the north coast of California. State Highway 1 runs along the coastline almost always within sight of the sea, and it is a drive of exceptional beauty. Another highly recommended trip in the area is aboard the *Super Skunk,* a splendid old California Western Railroad steam train that makes a two-hour serpentine run between Fort Bragg and Willits through the majestic redwood forests.

Not surprisingly, the area attracts a large number

Timeless garden flowers are always in style.

of tourists, too many for the relatively few really first-class accommodations in Mendocino. Hill House was constructed by Monte and Barbara Reed to meet that need. It took them six years to acquire permission from the State Coastal Commission to build their country inn; but when they were finished, they had created what would be unusual anywhere but in California—an instant classic.

HILL HOUSE OF MENDOCINO, 10701 Palette Dr., Mendocino, Calif. 95460; (707) 937-0554; Monte and Barbara Reed, Owners. Bob and Gert Permenter, Innkeepers. Although recently built, the inn was designed in perfect keeping with the architecture of this historic town, and the 21 guest rooms are furnished in Victorian décor. Private baths; phones, color TV. Rates, double and single, $46 to $65, including morning coffee and homemade coffee cake served in rooms. Each additional guest $5. A restaurant and bar is planned for the near future. Children welcome; no pets. No credit cards accepted. Shops and art galleries in town; many sports activities nearby.

DIRECTIONS: From San Francisco, take U.S. Rte. 101 to Rte. 128 at Cloverdale. Turn left to Rte. 1, then north to Mendocino. Take Main St. to Lansing, turn right to Palette Dr. and go right to inn.

A brand new country inn, both Victorian and modern inside and out, that anyone would enjoy.

Clapboard castle, New England style

For years, when Hollywood needed a small New England town for location shooting but couldn't afford to send a crew east, they would come to Mendocino, four hours north of San Francisco. Perched on cliffs above the Pacific Ocean, Mendocino was built in the 1850s by loggers, primarily from New England and Nova Scotia, who came to work the stand of redwoods by Big River. They knew how a proper town should look—precise and practical, plain and pretty.

One of the community's gems is the MacCallum House, built in 1882 by the father of the newly married Daisy MacCallum as a wedding present. She lived there for the next seventy-odd years, and the house is still filled with many of the original furnishings and MacCallum family memorabilia. Bill and Sue Norris, transplanted from the East via San Francisco, bought the well-kept house in 1974 and converted it into a country inn and restaurant. It is the kind of comfortable home that brings back memories of a childhood visit to a grandmother or favorite aunt's house.

One of the few new additions to the main house is the Grey Whale Bar, beautifully built by a local carpenter from golden and California oak. The restaurant

is a set of friendly rooms with dark-stained paneling and walls lined with the MacCallums' books. The menu is Continental and generally considered to be the best food in town.

The guest rooms in the main house are comfortable and cozy, and breakfast in bed is a tradition at MacCallum House. One of the largest, paneled in redwood, has a sleigh bed and a view of the town. Another has white wicker furniture, a delightful contrast to the bright wallpaper. Additional accommodations have been added in the newly renovated Greenhouse, snug and rustic, and the larger Carriage House, with five luxurious guest rooms, a loft for the children and a marvelous view of the cove from the living room. The Gazebo, a converted children's playhouse, is a charming miniature, but the bed is definitely large enough for grown-ups.

Mendocino's fiercely independent spirit reminds Bill of Nantucket, where he once had a summer home. Just as Nantucket and Martha's Vineyard recently tried to secede from Massachusetts, a group from Mendocino, outraged over some statewide environmental issues a few years ago, started a movement to secede from California. But Mendocino already is its own state. With so much natural beauty and comparative isolation, it is a truly distinctive and refreshing state of mind.

Distinguished pleasures of the table.

Wonder of wonders—a sunny sun porch called the Grey Whale Bar. OVERLEAF: the inn; a redwood paneled guest room with sleigh bed; breakfast in bed—a favorite pastime at the inn, and on the following pages, the town of Mendocino at sunset.

MacCALLUM HOUSE, P.O. Box 206, Mendocino, Calif. 95460; (707) 937-0289; Bill and Sue Norris, Innkeepers. A homey 24-room inn in a picturesque town on California's north coast. Shared baths. Open all year. Rates $34.50 to $65 double, including Continental breakfast. Restaurant serves dinner daily from April to Dec. Children welcome; no pets. Visa and Master Charge credit cards accepted. Sightseeing and shopping; tennis club in town.

DIRECTIONS: From San Francisco, take Route 101 to Cloverdale, exit onto Route 128 which leads into Route 1. Turn north to Mendocino 12 miles.

Where tourist and townsman meet

When Mendocino boomed as a lumber town in the last century, the headland on which it sits was crowded with houses right up to the edge of the cliffs, but time, fires and social change have altered the town drastically. Although many of today's residents in this picturesque cluster of frame houses on California's northern coast still earn their livelihood from forest and sea, others are artists and craftsmen.

One of the principal attractions of this little headland community is the Mendocino Hotel, built in 1878, which successfully combines yesterday's architectural tastes with today's lifestyle. Refurbished in 1973 from simple and somewhat shabby lodgings for loggers and traveling salesmen, the hotel now evokes a nostalgia for the rowdy gaudiness that characterized Mendocino in the nineteenth century when it was a rough lumberjack town. The plain, gold-colored false front is unchanged, and the interior is filled with turn-of-the-century oak, bright wallpaper and stained and beveled glass. Upstairs, the twenty-six guest rooms have canopied brass bedsteads that date from the 1880s to the 1920s and framed examples of early advertising art. Everything is keyed to comfort, and some of the accommodations have private baths. The enforced rearrangement of Mendocino's plan due to devastating fires considerably improved the hotel's view of both town and bay, and many of the rooms have balconies.

A glorious Tiffany glass dome from Philadelphia has been suspended over the carved wooden bar, a cheerful gathering place for a cross section of the town's social life. Tourists on holiday mingle easily with local artists and woodsmen, and the hotel's restaurant, which is open to the public, features local fish. Diners can choose to eat in the dining room, with its beveled glass, oak tables and chairs or, in nice weather, on the outdoor latticed terrace, where Mendocino's first fire engine is kept on display. A bright, plant-filled room has been added off the dining room, and the dark polished wood, Oriental rugs and flocked wallpapers all add to the sparkling Victorian atmosphere.

Art galleries and specialty shops in Mendocino offer good browsing, and a walk through town affords a fine prospect of the sometimes misty headlands and the weathered homes set amid flower gardens that bloom even in February.

The building has been totally renovated and decorated. Light, summery latticework is in some parts, as in the lounge at left. Heavier Victorian motifs are in the lobby, above.

MENDOCINO HOTEL, 45080 Main St., Mendocino, Calif. 95460; (707) 937-0511. A 26-room hotel, impeccably restored in the Victorian style. Private and shared baths. Open all year. Rates, including Continental breakfast, $25 to $60 double. One single room $26.50. Nov. through March, rates are $5 less. Elegant dining room and two popular bars. Children not encouraged; no pets. Visa and Master Charge credit cards accepted. Art galleries and specialty shops abound in this quaint New England-style village.

DIRECTIONS: From San Francisco, Mendocino is a 3½ hour drive. Take Coast Highway, Route 101 to 128, turn right onto Route 1. Exit onto Main St. in Mendocino. Inn is ½ mile on the right.

Handcrafted triumph, unique among inns

St. Orres is as much a triumph of the spirit as one of design. Its complex array of ornate domes is not, as one might expect, the work of the nineteenth-century Russian settlers in northern California, but the creation of two contemporary American master carpenters. Richard Wasserman and Eric Black bought a dilapidated fishing lodge and went to work. With the help of their friends, they built their own design around it, doing almost everything by hand, piece by piece, room by room. They were strongly influenced by the buildings constructed by Russian trappers in the late 1800s, but their creation went far beyond a nineteenth-century frontier house.

As do all good carpenters, Richard and Eric love the feel of a fine piece of wood. The inn's exterior is of Oregon red cedar, and the interiors are paneled in tongue-and-groove redwood. They are proud that many of the excellent materials used are recycled: the heavy frame of the inn itself is made from timbers salvaged from an old sawmill, and the copper on the domes is the discarded cladding of computer control equipment. Quality was an all-important consideration and construction was slow; but when they opened in 1977, Richard and Eric had one of the most unusual inns in America, with stunning visual effects both inside and out. A massive stone fireplace in the sitting room stands opposite a wall of six California oak doors, each with matching stained-glass windows made by a local craftsman. The dining room ends in a three-story tower with more stained glass encircling the dome. The eight guest rooms have redwood paneling in different geometric tongue-and-groove designs, and the built-in beds are covered with striking custom-made velvet quilts. Each guest room has a specially designed closet combining both chest and wardrobe. Even the telephone booth at St. Orres is paneled with redwood.

The food is excellent, and many visitors make the lovely drive all the way from San Francisco along the winding coast just for dinner. Others come for St. Orres' wonderful natural setting and feeling of isolation. Waves crash against the rocks in the craggy cove opposite the inn; and the inn's own beach, the next

Each of the guest rooms has recycled, tongue-and-groove redwood walls in varying designs. The quilts are handmade locally.

cove up, is a protected curve of sand at the mouth of a creek.

Eventually, the innkeeper-carpenters will build cabins in the thirty-five acres of redwood forest behind the inn, and the structures will be planned with the same deliberate care and mature imagination that went into St. Orres itself. No one plans to rush things.

The tower, with its dome and stained glass, is an exceptional place to dine on St. Orres' admirable food. OVERLEAF: the handmade inn, with its dining tower on the right.

ST. ORRES, P.O. Box 523, Gualala, Calif. 95445; (707) 884-3303; Eric Black, Rick Wasserman, Rosemary Campiformio, Ted Black, Innkeepers. A strikingly handsome 8-room inn on the north coast, lovingly built by hand by the proprietors. Shared baths. Rates $40 to $50 double or single, including Continental breakfast. Write or phone for reservations and rates in newly constructed cabins with fireplaces and private baths. Dining room open every day in summer except Tuesday; closed Wednesday through Sunday in winter. Sunday brunch. Children welcome; no pets. Visa and Master Charge credit cards accepted. Private beach. Hiking.

DIRECTIONS: On Route 1, 106 miles north of San Francisco, 2 miles north of Gualala.

A tub for two and vineyards in view

In 1870, Charles Rouvegneau came to Yountville, a sleepy little village settled in the 1830s, and built a small, sturdy fieldstone house similar to the ones in his native France. Rouvegneau made wine on the first floor and rented out the rooms upstairs. Over the years, the building was used for many things, not all of them respectable, and in 1975, Mary Keenan, a local antiques dealer, and her architect husband, Bob, took the place over for a shop. By then, the house had acquired a hundred years' worth of stucco, paint and plaster. Bob had everything sandblasted down to the original stone and wood, inside and out. When Mary opened her store, so many customers wanted to stay there that she was inspired to convert it into an inn. But Burgundy House is still an antiques shop, too, and guests have the unexpected pleasure of being able to live with something before actually buying it.

The Keenans are Francophiles, and French country antiques predominate. Their colorful personal touches include needlepoint Mary brought from Hong Kong, a chess set and other antique games plus a glorious cupboard hand-painted by a San Francisco artist. An upstairs bath has an antique shaving mirror, plants, an oversized tub with gold-painted claw feet, and a park bench for visiting. No clocks are to be found in the inn, as the Keenans feel that their guests shouldn't have to worry about time.

There is always a fire in the long common room in the winter, and in the summer the guests take their breakfast, the only meal served, out onto the secluded patio and enjoy the view across the Napa Valley vineyards to Mount Veeder in the distance. The guest rooms are bright and cheerful, with flower paintings hung on the stone walls. Some have elaborately carved Victorian bedsteads, others are antique iron or brass, set off with ruffled pillows, richly patterned comforters or silken sheets. Each guest room has its own decanter of Napa Valley wine, and there is always a selection of sherry, Burgundy and zinfandel for the guests in the common room. The accommodations have been expanded by a splendidly spacious suite in a store the Keenans remodeled across the street, and by a tiny house decorated in rich browns and reds.

The Napa Valley vineyards from the common room.
OVERLEAF: a colorful cupboard in one of the guest rooms and the famous tub for two.

The increasing interest in the Napa Valley vineyards has spawned several fine restaurants in the area, and champagne flights in a hot-air balloon from a nearby field offer a unique means of seeing the Napa Valley.

British conductor Neville Marriner once stayed here and said it reminded him of a snug little English inn, despite the profusion of French country antiques. It must be that the special warm atmosphere the Keenans have created makes all their guests feel welcome and at home no matter how far they have traveled.

BURGUNDY HOUSE COUNTRY INN, 6711 Washington St., Yountville, Calif. 94599; (707) 944-2711; Mary and Bob Keenan, Innkeepers. A 12-room inn in a Napa Valley wine country town. Six rooms in inn share baths; 6 rooms in 3 cottages with private baths. Open all year. Rates $55 to $60 double; $35 to $40 single, including Continental breakfast and wine. No dining room but list of recommended restaurants in area available. Children allowed in cottages; no pets. No credit cards accepted. Swimming pool, mineral baths, champagne balloon rides within 8 to 10 miles.

DIRECTIONS: From Route 29 take Yountville exit, drive north through town on Washington St. to inn.

Romantic and secluded, luxurious and indulgent

The playfully decorated lobby.

Bruce Locken, innkeeper at the Magnolia Hotel, has spent most of his life making guests comfortable in such places as the Casa Munras in Monterey and the Clift Hotel in San Francisco, where he was once general manager. Despite his high-powered background, Bruce has found his true happiness running the Magnolia Hotel, a small, seven-room establishment in Yountville. As Bruce explains, it is a case of "Why didn't we do this before?" The "we" includes Bonnie, who is Magnolia's chef and Bruce's wife, along with two sons and a daughter-in-law.

The Napa Valley is becoming an increasingly popular tourist attraction, and people come in growing numbers each year to see the vineyards and taste the wines. A good deal of the valley's appeal, however, has to do with the charm of such places as the Magnolia Hotel. Bonnie particularly cherishes a cookbook inscribed by Julia Child giving her enthusiastic approval of the meal she enjoyed at the Magnolia.

The bright red lampshade draped with tulle in the lobby may make guests think, at first, that they've stepped into a scene from *East of Eden,* but the abrupt little stairway leads to seven stylish guest rooms above, each with a private bath. "Everything we do is first class," says Bruce proudly. And everything is, from the marble-topped vanities to the magnolia-scented soap and sumptuously comfortable beds.

The smallest, most private room is on the third floor. "It's a favorite with couples on a second honeymoon," says Bonnie. A large bed fills practically all the space, and the window behind it has a view of the town. "When people stay up here," she says, "we find they seldom leave their room." When they do, it is probably for the splendid breakfast served at the large table in the dining room downstairs, where guests are treated to delicious French toast with a port wine syrup, one of Bonnie's creations.

Dinner at the Magnolia is served in an adjacent brick annex that the Lockens have decorated with great care. Chairs of white oak are placed at tables draped with lace cloths and set with the finest china and silver. Bonnie cooks a different meal each evening, usually featuring a classic French dish. Occasionally, she makes an exquisite chicken paprika, or a Viennese roast loin of pork.

The redwood deck behind the inn is a perfect place to relax and enjoy a soothing whirlpool spa in fenced-in privacy. The Locken's Siamese cats wander about with a proprietary air, and the all-pervasive mood of the Magnolia Hotel is at once romantic, secluded, luxurious and indulgent.

The elegant brick dining room in the annex.

MAGNOLIA HOTEL, 6529 Yount St., Yountville, Calif. 94599; (707) 944-2056; Bruce and Bonnie Locken, Innkeepers. A 7-room hotel dating from 1873 in the Napa Valley wine country. Private baths. Open all year. Rates are $48 to $65 double, including complete breakfast. Complimentary decanter of wine in each room. Restaurant serves lavish 5-course dinner Thursday through Sunday by reservation only. Extensive wine cellar features more than 250 varieties of California wine. No children under 12; no pets. No credit cards accepted. Swimming pool and heated jacuzzi. Boutiques, art galleries, wineries and balloon rides nearby.

DIRECTIONS: From Route 29, take Yountville exit, drive north on Washington St., which continues into Yountville St. Hotel is on the left.

Victorian elegance, Western style

Sonoma County lays claim to being the "cradle of California history," and Russian, English, Mexican, Spanish and American flags have flown over the region at various times. The northernmost mission in Alta California, then under Mexican control, was built here in 1823 and was the site for the town of Sonoma, founded several years later.

The hotel was probably built somewhere around 1872, but it was used for various purposes before becoming a hotel in 1920. The present-day innkeepers, John and Dorene Musilli, bought it in 1974 and set about restoring the hotel to a proper nineteenth-century hostelry, refurnished with authentic items from the days of the Barbary Coast and the Gay Nineties. The building, with adobe infill, was structurally sound; but inside, the banisters and trim had to be laboriously stripped of eight layers of paint to get down to the wood. The two etched-glass panels in the double front doors give a proper Western touch to the entrance, and the main sitting room is a warm gathering place looking out on the town square. The hotel has seventeen distinctive guest rooms. Room 3 is furnished with a rosewood bedroom suite, on loan from the Sonoma League for Historic Preservation, that once belonged to an illustrious resident of Sonoma, General Vallejo, the governor of Alta California. Room 2 offers a five-piece suite made of hand-carved wood and rare orange marble, and another guest room contains a suite of solid oak inlaid with ebony. There are several fine brass bedsteads, and Room 29 features an enchanting pair of hand-carved Austrian children's beds, a French dresser with its original tin mirror and a graceful chandelier.

The adobe relics of early Sonoma are everywhere around the town plaza. The old mission is located on one corner, and on the north side is the Mexican Soldiers' Barracks and the restored but nonfunctioning Hotel Toscano. Down the street is the Blue Wing Inn, built by General Vallejo in 1840 and now made over into antique shops. The Blue Wing's guest book

An exotic brass bed dominates Room 1.

The lobby set for breakfast of croissants and coffee.

shows visits from such Wild West personalities as John C. Frémont, Kit Carson and the bandit Joaquin Murietta.

Sonoma also lays claim to another very important event in California history. A young Hungarian nobleman, Agoston Haraszthy, had spent ten years searching the new continent for soil comparable to that in his homeland suitable for viniculture, and he finally found what he was looking for in Sonoma. In 1855, he bought 500 acres just east of town, which he planted with cuttings from Europe. With this first planting, the California wine industry was born.

SONOMA HOTEL, 110 West Spain St., Sonoma, Calif. 95476; (707) 996-2996; John and Dorene Musilli, Innkeepers. A 17-room hotel in a historic town in the wine country. Shared baths. Open all year. Rates $32 to $49 double; $30 to $44 single, including Continental breakfast. Children welcome; no pets. Visa, Master Charge and American Express credit cards accepted. Sightseeing in historic town; visits to local wineries.

DIRECTIONS: From San Francisco, take I-101 to Route 37 at Vallejo. Turn off Route 37 onto 121 to Sonoma. Hotel is on northwest corner of the town plaza.

Solar energy.

Sunlight filters through the lobby curtains. The etched-glass design on the front door, below right, lends a western feeling. The historic district adjacent to the plaza is a very pleasant place to stroll.

Taste and style in a classic mold

Stone terraces lead downhill from this charming country inn to a patio edged with olive trees. A series of balconies offers sweeping views of the valley and the hills beyond. Chinese pistachios grow along the driveway, and even in January daisies bloom by the outside stair. The stone tower, the distinctive roof lines, the walls of board and batten are reminiscent of Continental Europe and have a definite flavor of the style of building in the early days in the Napa Valley. The settlers who came over in the second half of the nineteenth century, many of whom helped start the California vineyards, would feel very comfortable here. The Wine Country Inn looks as if it had long been part of the landscape, and it is a surprise to learn it was only built in 1975.

Ned and Marge Smith had always wanted to be innkeepers, and for years they spent their vacations at inns in the British Isles, New England and the West, gathering ideas for their own inn. When they were at last ready to build, they went to an artist, instead of an architect, who sketched their inn exactly the way they wanted it. Then they designed the rooms to conform to the overall plan, purposely giving each one a significant feature of its own, such as a balcony or a patio or even a fireplace. The result is an inn with all the character and style of the nineteenth century combined with the sophisticated comforts of the twentieth.

The common room is a large comfortable area paneled in barn siding, with comfortable sofas and chairs, an iron stove and a long English harvest table where breakfast is served. The Smiths were active in the interior decoration, too, and Marge made many of the lovely quilts for the handsome guest rooms. All have been distinctively decorated, one in red, white and blue, another with twin headboards made of wine-cask bases. The Smiths thoughtfully widened a Victorian headboard so it could accommodate a king-size mattress.

A canopied extravaganza.

A leisurely breakfast is the only meal served at the inn, but there are a number of fine restaurants in the area. A selection of their menus is kept on the table in the common room for guests to look through, and the Smiths will make the reservations. Guests are invited to keep their wines in the inn's refrigerator, and a cupboard in the common room is kept well stocked with glasses.

It is this kind of personal attention to detail that contributes to the rich heritage of hospitality in a country inn. After only four years, Ned and Marge Smith are already innkeepers in the classic mold.

WINE COUNTRY INN, 1152 Lodi Lane, St. Helena, Calif. 94574; (707) 963-7077; Ned and Marge Smith and Jim Smith, Innkeepers. A stunning 25-room inn built in the style of early Napa Valley buildings. Private baths. Open all year. Rates $47 to $65 double. Single $3 less. Rates include buffet-style Continental breakfast, the only meal served. Children over 12 welcome; no pets. Visa and Master Charge credit cards accepted. Nearby wineries open to visitors.

DIRECTIONS: Route 29 through Napa Valley. North of St. Helena, 2 miles, turn at sign for Lodi Lane. Inn's entrance just down the road on left.

The driveway up to the inn is lined with oaks. OVERLEAF: Napa Valley in January. *A view of the inn building appears on page 1.*

Centerpiece of a museum town

Two brothers struck gold in 1850 in what turned out to be the heart of the California Mother Lode. Within a month, some six thousand miners were working the area; and by the time they were done, some $87 million worth of gold had been extracted from the Columbia field. As the mining camp grew from tents to a proper town, the miners felt they needed a little class in their public establishments, and in 1856 the What Cheer House was built. It was rebuilt in 1867 after a fire, along with much of the rest of town, and was renamed the City Hotel in 1874.

In its time, the building has been a newspaper office, the local opera house and an assay office, but it was as a tavern and hotel that it was best known. Now, as the result of a massive restoration project by the State of California, it is once again in business and is the focal point of the Columbia State Historic Park. The entire community is a working museum of the exciting Gold Rush days, and the town is so well preserved it is often used for filming TV westerns. The City Hotel, like most of Columbia, is built of brick and has an iron filigree balustrade around its second-story balcony. French doors on the ground floor are flanked by heavy iron shutters, which at one time served the double purpose of fire control and protection against boisterous miners. The rooms are well-proportioned, Victorian but not especially western, with the exception of the What Cheer Saloon. Many of the miners were homesick easterners who had solid Victorian furniture brought overland by wagon or around Cape Horn by ship. The rooms at the City Hotel would delight them today, and of the nine guest rooms, Room 1 is the star. It has its own balcony door, and the massive carved walnut bedstead is supposed to have belonged to the warden of San Quentin Prison. The rooms have their own half-baths, and guests shower down the hall following the nineteenth-century custom.

The hotel's chef came from Ernie's, one of San Francisco's finest restaurants. The French and international cuisine would flabbergast the old miners, used to beef jerky and cheap whiskey, who certainly

Gold Rush days brought back to life in the guest rooms.

couldn't have spelled *chateaubriand* and wouldn't have known what it was, anyway.

Thanks to the farsightedness of the State of California, what might have been a ghost town in the Gold Rush Sierra country is very much alive, and the City Hotel is the perfect base for visiting this fascinating area that has seen so much of California's history.

CITY HOTEL, Main Street, Columbia, Calif. 95310; (209) 532-1479; Tommy Bender, Innkeeper. A 9-room hotel in a re-created Gold Rush town. Private half-baths, with shower down the hall. Open all year except Christmas. Rates $33.50 to $42.50 double, including Continental breakfast. Restaurant, offering fine French cuisine and vintage wines, serves lunch daily except Sunday and Monday; dinner except Monday. Children welcome; no pets. Visa and Master Charge credit cards accepted. Hotel is the focal point of a handsomely restored Mother Lode town in Columbia State Historic Park. What Cheer Saloon in hotel; Sierra Railroad nearby.

DIRECTIONS: Three hours' drive from San Francisco, hotel is 3 miles north of Sonora on Route 49. Hotel is on Main St., closed to traffic during the day in summer. In winter, Main St. open 5 P.M. to 8 A.M. Take alternate road around town center and park in back of hotel.

The dining room, restored to its former glory. OVERLEAF: the building's façade and, on the following pages, two views of other restorations in Columbia's commercial district. *Left*, the Wells Fargo office and *right*, the familiar corner filmed in many westerns.

A lively inn in a historic site

The thick-walled, two-story adobe that Dr. Louis Gunn built on Washington Street in 1851 was one of Sonora's few substantial buildings at that time. Serving as Dr. Gunn's home and the office of the local newspaper, the *Sonora Herald,* that he also ran, the building was the focus of political controversy in the 1850s when Dr. Gunn defended the civil rights of Chinese laborers. An outspoken liberal from Philadelphia, Dr. Gunn so angered the local citizenry that they once hauled his printing press onto the street and incinerated it. Dr. Gunn moved to San Francisco in 1861; and as Sonora expanded over the years, so did his old house. Eventually, the original adobe was only one section of a long balconied building that served for a time as a hospital, then as the city hall and, finally, as a hotel.

Its present good looks are the result of a restoration and expansion undertaken by Mrs. Margaret Dienelt

in the 1960s. The now three-story Gunn House climbs the steep hill on which it is built, and at the back a beautiful stone terrace has been laid out around an oval swimming pool. Whether in the old adobe section, or in one of the newer rooms overlooking the pool, the Gunn House offers an exemplary way of life in this bracing, yet sometimes hot, climate.

An interior courtyard provides the focus for the sprawling complex, and its wrought-iron grillwork recalls the town's early Mexican heritage. Just off the courtyard there is a parlor with a stone floor and extravagant Victorian furnishings, complete with a gilt-framed mirror and a pedal organ in one corner. Much of the décor of the twenty-seven rooms, all with their own baths, is also Victorian, with many walnut and mahogany mirrored vanities that graze the ceiling.

There's a lively holiday spirit at the Gunn House, since guests are apt to be just starting their vacation or just finishing one. Among the many local sights are the Sierra Railroad at nearby Jamestown and several Gold Rush towns. The Gunn House is a living link that gives a new generation of visitors a real feeling of California's fabulous past.

The color coordinated swimming pool.

The entrance lobby, restored and elegantly furnished.

THE GUNN HOUSE, 286 South Washington St., Sonora, Calif. 95370; (209) 532-3421; Peggy Schoell, Innkeeper. A 27-room inn expanded and restored from an 1850s adobe house. Located in a Gold Rush town in the Sierra foothills. Private baths. Open all year. Rates, including morning coffee and rolls, from $23 to $34 double, depending on sleeping accommodations. No restaurant. Children welcome; pets accepted at innkeeper's discretion. Visa and Master Charge credit cards accepted. Swimming pool, TV in each guest room; Columbia State Park and Sierra Railroad 3 miles away.

DIRECTIONS: Take Route 49 to Sonora. Inn is on right just south of town center on Route 108 (South Washington Street).

Golden elegance in the Mother Lode

The neat, rather elegant brick building, with its white pillared porch, is set on a hill overlooking the tiny Mother Lode settlement of Amador City. It once belonged to the Keystone Consolidated Mine and shares a hillside with the ruins of the original stamping mill. After the mine closed in 1942, the future of the old building was doubtful until the Daubenspeck family bought it in 1948 and converted it into an inn.

"The early owners of the mine had Southern connections," says innkeeper Peter Daubenspeck III, "and the mine offices were pretty obviously designed in a variant of the Southern Plantation-style." A wide, white-painted board fence climbs the hill to The Mine House, and in spring, daffodils bloom in profusion.

The Daubenspecks have treated what they found with great respect. Most of the private baths have been fitted into what were originally large closets. One room has a shower built into an arched brick structure that supports the vault where the heavy safe that held gold bullion still stands.

Furnishings in the beautifully kept inn are almost all Victorian pieces found locally. As a whimsical tribute to the necessities of yesteryear, a china chamber pot is placed at the foot of each bed. On the walls are engravings and popular art from the late nineteenth century. In the Retort Room, where $23 million in gold was smelted into bullion, a quaintly framed wall plaque reads Charity Never Faileth. The typically Victorian high ceiling of the Director's Room is intact, and sheer curtains give a soft romantic look to the Keystone Room.

The prospect of the town below from the rocking chairs on the front veranda, and the more secluded

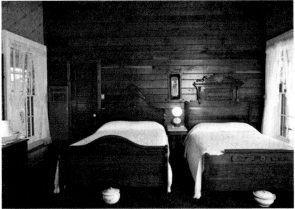

The converted guest rooms are charming.

porch in back adjacent to a sun-screened terrace, with a view up the hill to the magnificent trees and meadow, would make any guest want to linger. The press of a button in the morning will bring juice and coffee to a guest's bedroom door, and a pool offers a refreshing respite after a day of sightseeing in the Gold Rush country.

Not all the gold is gone. According to the Daubenspecks, the vein was far from exhausted when the mine was closed, but the cost of getting it out now would be prohibitive. All the same, it's nice to think of gold hiding there under the hill, a reminder of the prosperous past.

THE MINE HOUSE INN, Amador City, Calif. 95601; (209) 267-5900; Peter Daubenspeck III, Innkeeper. An 8-room inn in a former mine headquarters building in a tiny gold town. Private baths. Open all year. Rates $24 to $29 double; $20 to $29 single, including breakfast, fruit juice and coffee or tea. No restaurant. Children welcome; no pets. No credit cards accepted. Swimming pool. Antique and craft shops, wine tasting room in town; restaurants nearby.

DIRECTIONS: On Route 49, 2 miles north of Sutter Creek.

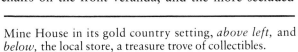

Mine House in its gold country setting, *above left*, and *below*, the local store, a treasure trove of collectibles.

Comfort and tradition in a boom-town hostelry

"I love the color burgundy," says Dick Ness, proprietor of California's oldest continuously operating hotel. "It's pretty hard to like the National if you *don't* like the color burgundy." No son of the Sierras, Dick is originally a flatlander from the San Francisco Bay Area, but he has developed a feeling for the style of the hills that includes a liberal use of bright color, usually red. The National, which first opened in 1854, is anything but pure in style. It occupies four adjoining brick buildings on Nevada City's Broad Street. Nothing in the hotel is just as it once was: an annex has come and gone; the present lobby—on the second floor—was once the ballroom. The bar was moved to its street-level location sometime in the 1920s and embellished with a lavish piece of woodwork from the Spreckels mansion in San Francisco.

As the major hostelry of one of California's gold towns, the hotel has entertained generations of merchants, speculators and visitors in high style. Many of its thirty guest rooms have curtained alcoves and wide, ornate Victorian bedsteads, and much of the furniture still has the stiff, store-bought opulence of a frontier town that has struck it rich. A few longtime guests use the lobby as their living room. It is both grand and homelike, with chandeliers, Victorian sofas and oak armchairs. Hotel personnel bustle about, arranging a wedding reception, checking reservations for a couple coming in from Tokyo or maybe just talking about the previous evening's meeting of the VFW Auxiliary.

Now an extravagantly furnished lobby—
formerly the ballroom.

French doors in the lobby open onto a terrace that provides a dramatic prospect of the quirky, charming town. Built on hills with random and precipitous streets, Nevada City still boasts many buildings from the boom days, including a beautiful theater—California's oldest—where Lola Montez, Oscar Wilde and Sarah Bernhardt appeared. Down the street, the American Victorian Museum houses a collection of artifacts from the area that reveals the exuberance of the young, thriving frontier. Nevada City was cut out of the wilderness, and beyond the town are the forests and hills that once drew thousands of gold-hungry prospectors who came to make their fortune.

Today, visitors and settlers can still reap a fortune in unpolluted air and Victorian charm. "When I first got here," says Dick Ness, "all I wanted was a cabin on a lake. I ended up with the National. I guess it's the atmosphere of the hills. You may think crazy, but at least you think big."

Old-time, store-bought opulence.

The National Hotel hasn't stopped since 1854.

NATIONAL HOTEL, 211 Broad St., Nevada City, Calif. 95959; (916) 265-4551; Dick and Nan Ness, Innkeepers. A 30-room hotel, with Western-style saloon and Victorian dining room, in a former Sierra gold mining town. Private baths. Open all year. Rates $24 double, with double bed; $25 double, with twin beds; suites $35 to $40. No breakfast served but there are several good restaurants nearby, including one at the American Victorian Museum that should not be missed. The hotel dining room, featuring an extensive and varied Continental menu, is highly recommended for lunch, dinner and Sunday brunch. Children welcome; no pets. Visa and Master Charge credit cards accepted. Swimming pool, saloon, TV. Antique and craft shops, historic buildings nearby.

DIRECTIONS: From Sacramento, take Route I-80 to Auburn, then Route 49 to Broad St. turnoff. Left on Broad St. across Deer Creek. Hotel is on the left.

Informal comfort in welcoming spaces

The breakfast room.

Sutter Creek is fifty miles south of the famous spot in the American River where a carpenter discovered gold flakes in the water near the sawmill owned by John Sutter. It is a quiet town with many restored buildings and simple, wooden Gold Rush homes painted blue, red and yellow. The Sutter Creek Inn was built in 1859 by one of the town's leading merchants for his New Hampshire bride, and it started out as a Greek Revival cottage. The addition of an ell, a front porch and various outbuildings gave it its own distinctive flair, and it is typical of many homes that grew and expanded to serve the needs of successive owners.

Jane Way chanced on it in 1966 when she was on a trip through the Gold Rush country with her children. It had been empty for some time, and she fell in love with it on sight. There were a few snags, but she bought it and converted it into a country inn. The house is filled with her family's furniture and the results of her own extensive antiquing forays. The living room has two sofas flanking the fireplace with a sled-topped coffee table between, a beautiful big hutch from Boston and a large chest from Quebec.

Breakfast is a major event, served at nine o'clock sharp in the huge, eat-in kitchen. Jane whacks a big gong, and she and her staff cook up platters of eggs, pancakes and muffins. If any guests are late, they've lost out, but the aroma of fresh coffee and hot breads usually gets most people up willingly. If anyone is hungry again by lunchtime, or even by dinnertime, Jane provides a list of local restaurants that includes her own capsule reviews.

Jane has expanded the accommodations by converting the old service buildings, each keeping the name of its original function: Upper Washhouse, Cellar Room, Woodshed and Miner's Cabin. Each house is different, reflecting Jane's wide-ranging tastes, and the grounds are landscaped with walk-ways, little gardens and shade trees providing a peaceful retreat. Most unusual at Sutter Creek Inn are the swinging beds, an idea Jane got from a friend, which combines a bed with a hammock. They can be made stationary, but most people love the gently rocking motion.

"Once you get used to them," says Jane, "they're much more comfortable than water beds. I'd give them about two nights."

SUTTER CREEK INN, 75 Main St., Sutter Creek, Calif. 95685; (209) 267-5606; Jane Way, Innkeeper. An 18-room inn in a Gold Rush village. Private and shared baths. Open all year except Jan. Rates $30 to $65 double, depending on particular room and whether accommodations are for midweek or weekend. Carriage House $55; $65 on weekends and holidays. Rates include full breakfast for guests only, the only meal served. Coffee, tea and brandy served before breakfast. Children over 15 welcome; no pets. No credit cards accepted. Croquet, hammocks, swings. Picturesque town, interesting shops, excellent restaurants.

DIRECTIONS: Located 50 miles east of Sacramento on Route 49, 3 miles north of Jackson.

OVERLEAF: *Left*: Sutter Creek's Victorian bay window aflame with Pyracanth berries. *Right*: R. W. Tyler, a local gallery owner, has also written a *Stroller's Guide to Sutter Creek*.

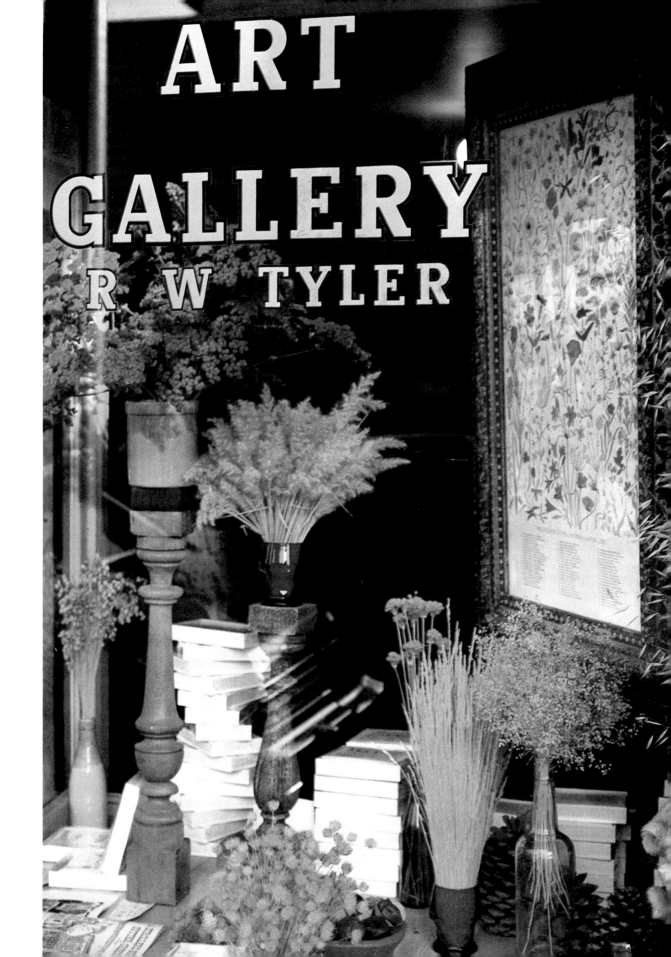

The rooms are all different and all beautiful.

A country hideaway in the heart of a city

A country inn is sometimes as much a matter of style as it is of location. Compared to the usual run of impersonal city hotels, the Bed and Breakfast Inn in San Francisco seems like a Napa Valley hideaway. It is a tiny place on Charlton Court, just off Union Street, with only seven rooms and the best San Francisco has to offer.

Innkeepers Bob and Marily Kavanaugh are transplanted from Southern California, and every detail shows that running the Bed and Breakfast Inn is a labor of love for them. The front door is practically enveloped in foliage, and there are fresh flowers in the common room and the guest rooms, as well. Three rooms open onto a lovely garden's profusion of colorful flowers, and one secluded spot is a peaceful, monochromatic Japanese garden. Some of the rooms have such evocative names as Kensington Garden, Green Park and Willows. Autumn Sun is subdued and restful. The charming frame building next door contains three minisuites, each with its own distinctive character and each more spectacular than the last. Sydney

Greenstreet would approve of The Mandalay, with lots of rattan, a chair with a peacock fan back, a ceiling fan and mosquito netting over the large comfortable bed. Covent Gardens sports a latticework arcade framing a riot of flowers, and Celebration has a sunken tub.

English prints are hung in the common room, and the best china is used for a leisurely breakfast of coffee, juice, buttery croissants and jam. A flower-bedecked tray will be brought to guests who want breakfast in bed; and if champagne is required for some special occasion, it comes in a silver bucket.

For the Kavanaughs, keeping everything shining and blooming is more than a full-time job, but the satisfactions are "incredible," according to Marily. Pinned on her bulletin board in the kitchen is a quote from actress Ruth Gordon: "Never give up, and never, under any circumstances, no matter what, ever face the facts."

The flower-fringed life at the Bed and Breakfast Inn proves that some fantasies make it in the real world.

Breakfast can be had in the common room, *above*, in bed, or on the terrace.

BED AND BREAKFAST INN, 4 Charlton Court, San Francisco, Calif. 94123; (415) 921-9784; Robert and Marily Kavanaugh, Innkeepers. A 7-room inn, with charming gardens, in a secluded court off San Francisco's boutique-lined Union St. Open all year. Rates $32 to $52 double, without private bath; $74 to $94 double, with bath. Single, 10% discount. Rates include Continental breakfast. No other meals served. Children not encouraged; no pets. No credit cards accepted. Some rooms have TV and there is a set in the Library, open to all guests. Reservations are essential and are accepted no more than 2 months in advance.

DIRECTIONS: From Union Square, San Francisco, go west on Sutter St. to Franklin St. Turn right on Franklin and proceed to Union St. Turn left on Union to Charlton Court, on left-hand side of Union between Laguna and Buchanan.

Italianate mansion into Continental hotel

In 1885, William Barrett, a transplanted Vermonter who had made a fortune in lumbering, built his dream house on the hillsides of Sausalito. It was an Italianate Victorian pile, with marble fireplaces, stained-glass windows and extensive iron grillwork, set in an impressive terraced garden overlooking San Francisco Bay. Barrett's villa became the showplace of a community of gracious homes.

As is often the case with fine old nineteenth-century houses, Casa Madrona went somewhat to seed after its original owners departed. For a while it was used as a hotel, an inn and, if local rumor is correct, even as a bordello. During the 1950s, it became a community crash pad for members of the beatnik generation. Restoration of the old place was begun in the 1960s by Robert Henri Deschamps, a restaurateur with a fine sense of Continental elegance. He leased the hotel and installed Le Vivoir, a French restaurant of such excellence that San Franciscans, who know something of fine cuisine, immediately declared it one of the premier establishments in the Bay Area. Le Vivoir's sumptuous Cuisine Bourgeoise has attracted a worldwide following for its specialties, such as pigeons de Berville, veau St. Armour and lapin Braconnier, served in a charming candlelit room with a spectacular view of the yacht harbor below.

John Mays, an attorney with the eye of an artist, discovered the Casa Madrona in 1976 and bought the establishment. With Deschamps still running Le Vivoir on the first floor, Mays set about restoring the upstairs rooms to their original grandeur.

The result is a splendid California hotel with the warmth and style of a European country inn. Each of the accommodations, including a separate guest house, is a creation with its own name and personality. The Gingham Room is delightfully Victorian in cheery blue and white, while the Mariner Room features nautical touches in a sturdy setting of natural redwood and brick. The Fireside Room still has the original mahogany fireplace and a sweeping view of the harbor, while the Royal Room offers an impressive king-size canopied brass bed. Guests may be reminded of Casa Madrona's giddier days in the Barbary Coast Room.

All the rooms are restored to their original grandeur, with comfortable additions.

A spectacular view.

But whichever room they select, guests will find that after almost one hundred years, the Casa Madrona is once again what it started out to be—a dream house.

CASA MADRONA HOTEL, 156 Bulkley Ave., Sausalito, Calif. 94965; (415) 332-0502; John W. Mays, Innkeeper. A magnificently restored 1885 mansion overlooking yacht harbor. Fourteen rooms, all but 4 with private baths, and 4 cottages each accommodating 4 persons. Rooms have either double beds or king or queen size beds. Rollaway bed available for additional guest. Open all year. Rates, including Continental breakfast in sitting room, from $32 to $60. Wine with cheese and crackers served in sitting room before dinner, available in the elegant Le Vivoir restaurant, on the first floor, featuring a celebrated French cuisine bourgeoise. Other restaurants in nearby downtown Sausalito. Children welcome. Pets allowed in cottages. Visa, Master Charge and American Express credit cards accepted. Interesting browsing in nearby art galleries and craft shops.

DIRECTIONS: A ½-hour ferry ride across the bay from San Francisco; by car, take Route 101 over Golden Gate Bridge. Take first exit after bridge (Alexander Ave.) to downtown Sausalito. At first traffic light turn left on Princess St. Bear right up hill on Bulkley Ave. to hotel on right-hand side.

PHOTOGRAPHED BY DENNIS DUGGAN

International flavor in a seaside inn

Pacific Grove, on California's beautiful Monterey Peninsula, began as a Methodist retreat whose residents lived in tents. As the town's imposing Victorian architecture testifies, however, the good townsmen soon wanted more elaborate accommodations. The Gosby House Inn on Lighthouse Avenue is a particularly fine example of their elevated taste in architecture. Built of redwood, turreted and gabled in the fashion of the 1880s, the Gosby House Inn was the result of a local handyman's bid for the visitors who came to bathe or to be uplifted by the lectures.

By the time Roger and Sally Post came upon it, however, it had become a shabby establishment whose fortunes had not survived Pacific Grove's evolution from a nineteenth-century camp to a modern resort community. The Posts, with the help of young hotel man Bill Patterson, began a complete restoration. Dropped ceilings were removed to reveal exquisite plaster rosettes in the original ceiling above; stripping and cleaning disclosed elaborate patterns in the brass hardware. Slowly, the fine old mansion began to reappear.

When the basic restoration had been finished, Bill began to think about furniture. For more than a month, he lived in the house, sleeping in each guest room "to find out what it needed, what kind of bed, how it should be placed." He brought in European-style furnishings from the turn of the century, a time

when the popularity of the Gosby House Inn was at its height, to create a California inn with an international flavor.

The predominant color scheme is light and airy, and white ruffled curtains temper the strong sunlight of the seaside town. Each room is named for a prominent local figure; guests may choose the Robert Louis Stevenson Room or the John Steinbeck Room. Whatever the accommodation, it will be distinctive, because the eccentric construction of the house has created rooms with odd corners and projecting bays. Perhaps the most dramatic is the turret room, with a curving window wall that affords a view toward the water over the lower town. Guests enjoy a Continental breakfast in the common room, with its heavy, dark oak table and Queen Anne chairs. In a huge armoire, Sally Post has arranged a delightful collection of antique dolls.

Pacific Grove, with its wealth of Victorian cottages set amid blooming gardens, combines nineteenth-century charm with enough present-day excitement to please a whole new generation of visitors who could not do better than to put up at the Gosby House Inn.

THE GOSBY HOUSE INN, 643 Lighthouse Ave., Pacific Grove, Calif. 93950; (408) 375-1287; Bill Patterson, Innkeeper. A charming architectural oddity, with 18 rooms, in a Victorian seaside community on Monterey Bay. Private and shared baths. Open all year. Rates, including Continental breakfast, $25 to $40 double. No restaurant, but menus for area restaurants available for guests' convenience. Children not encouraged; no pets. No credit cards accepted. Inn is 6 blocks from the ocean. Golfing, tennis and sailing nearby.

DIRECTIONS: South of Monterey on Route 1, take Pebble Beach-Pacific Grove exit onto Route 68 West, which becomes Forest Ave. Proceed on Forest to Lighthouse Ave. Turn left on Lighthouse 3 blocks to inn at 18th Street.

The turret room.

A corner of the common room, with Mrs. Post's collection of antique dolls.

The pool terrace.

Fantasy inn in a treasure town

Style has always been important in Carmel. How could it be otherwise in a village where the main street ends at the Pacific Ocean, on a wide strand, with splendid surf and a view of the spectacular headland of Point Lobos? The town began as an artists' community, with plain shingled cottages among the pines. A few of these charming and primitive accommodations still serve today as part of the Normandy Inn, but the main house itself is a picturesque example of French country-style architecture added to the English cottages, Spanish courtyards and Swiss chalets of Carmel. Heavy wood struts support casement windows; shingle roofs crown turretlike projections; brick and stone walkways bordered with flowers lead up, down and all around the complex, dotted with topiary art and espaliered trees. The paved courtyards are showpieces of design, especially one with a splendid timber staircase winding up to a second-story balcony. A rock-rimmed swimming pool graces a secluded terrace. The atmosphere is that of a solid and substantial French country inn, and many of the rooms have beds tucked in niches, and fireplaces faced with glazed tile. The newer accommodations have king-size beds and picture windows, and most of the cottages have their own kitchenettes.

The Normandy Inn is fantasy architecture, readily admits its designer, architect Robert Stanton, whose son Mike is now innkeeper. But like many of California's fantasies, it works.

Nearby is the Seventeen-Mile Drive, where twisted Monterey cypresses, coastal pines, rocks, ocean and cliffs provide a setting for a string of estates on what has been called America's Riviera. There are beautifully groomed golf courses, and, for the less athletic, an almost unending number of art galleries and specialty shops offer untold treasures. It would seem all the marine paintings, all the jade jewelry and all the figurines and miniatures to be had in the world are displayed right here.

In a village of splendid extremes, the Normandy Inn is quite at home.

NORMANDY INN, Carmel, Calif. 93921; (408) 624-3825; Samuel M. Stanton, Innkeeper. A 45-room French Provincial-style inn in a unique resort village by the sea. Includes cottage rooms, some with fireplaces and kitchenettes. Also 3 charming and typical Carmel cottages accommodating up to 8 guests. Rates are $30 to $48, double, including Continental breakfast. No other meals served. Children welcome; no pets. No credit cards accepted. TV in newer guest rooms; heated swimming pool; 3 blocks from ocean beach; art galleries, shops, restaurants and golf courses nearby, including famed Pebble Beach.

DIRECTIONS: Take Route 1 south of Monterey to Carmel turnoff for Ocean Ave. Inn is on left between Monteverde and Casanova just past downtown shopping area.

A very French atmosphere.

Cherished family home, gracious country inn

Most people, when their children grow up and start living on their own, begin to think about moving into a smaller home and taking it easy. But not Gene and Ann Swett. When one after another of their six children moved away from the Swetts' ample Tudor-style home, they took in foreign exchange students to fill each gap.

"This has always been a very special house," says Ann. "It is the sort of place where strangers arrive at the door and ask if they can come in to look around. We just like to have it filled all the time."

And so the Swetts decided to go all the way and convert their home into a small inn. First, they toured the state, visiting other inns in order to pick and choose among their favorite features. They opened in September 1978, and the Old Monterey Inn quickly became known as a gracious country inn that could stand comparison with the finest in the area.

Each of the eight guest rooms has its own distinctive flair and stylistic touches, whether it's an old-fashioned swinging bed suspended from the ceiling or a small brick fireplace. Staying at the Old Monterey Inn is like visiting with old friends. "We live in the back now," Ann explains. "Our guests use our living room and dining room as their own. Of course, when there is a really big football game on television, everyone seems to end up sitting with us in the kitchen."

The Swetts pamper their guests the way they did their children. In the evening, they serve quantities of homemade cheeses along with the best of California sherry. But the principal occasion at the Old Monterey Inn is the informal breakfast. Guests may have it brought to their rooms on a tray or they may join the others in front of the fire in the dining room. When the weather is particularly fine, as it often is, they can take their trays out into the garden. Whatever they do, they will be starting out the day on a particularly happy note. Ann describes breakfast with some understatement as "generous." Fragrant hot coffee and freshly squeezed orange juice topped with banana slices are served along with breads straight from Ann's kitchen, fruit compotes and cheese. Every breakfast also features a selection of at least three different kinds of pastries brought in daily from the local baker.

"It's a terrible decision to decide on which one," says Ann.

Terrible, but somehow the guests at the Old Monterey Inn manage to survive.

One of the newly decorated guest rooms.

OLD MONTEREY INN, 500 Martin St., Monterey, Calif. 93940, (408) 375-8284; Gene and Ann Swett, Innkeepers. Handsome Tudor-style family home, now an 8-room inn in one of California's most scenic areas. Private and semi-private baths. Open all year. An exceptionally generous Continental breakfast is the only meal served. Rates $50 to $65 single or double. Children over 16 welcome; no pets. No credit cards accepted. All popular sports facilities nearby; deep-sea fishing, whale watching; 5 minutes from picturesque Carmel; short drive to John Steinbeck's Cannery Row and the famed 17-Mile Drive.

DIRECTIONS: From San Francisco take Route 1 to Monterey Peninsula exit north of Salinas. This joins Route 1 in Castroville. Take Monterey exit from Route 1 to Abrego, turn left and proceed to El Dorado. Turn right to Pacific, left ½ block, then right on Martin St. 1 block to inn.

PHOTOGRAPHED BY JIM PECK

Clocks are everywhere.

A garden retreat Western style

The heart of this romantic hideaway—its outdoor living room—is the plant-filled garden courtyard shaded by two California live oaks. Gigantic staghorn ferns, tree fuchsias, camellia bushes and cyclamens flourish, and the permanent evergreens provide a background for the seasonal floral changes.

Built in 1941 as a series of efficiency apartments and converted to an inn in 1947, Vagabond House presents itself from the outside as a group of neat white stucco cottages built into the side of a gently rising hill. A curving path leads up into the courtyard in the center of the complex.

Innkeepers Dennis Levett and Jewell Brown have redecorated the rooms with new rugs and bedspreads and supplemented the original collection of antiques with many fine examples of their own, particularly in a handsome new lobby enhanced by a magnificent oriental rug. Every room has one or more clocks, many of them collector's pieces.

The guest rooms are spacious and all have private baths. Some have fireplaces; others have kitchens.

On the beach.

Every room either opens directly onto the garden or overlooks it. The inn is open all year, and many guests settle in for a week, a month or a whole season. Each room is decorated in an individual and sometimes whimsical style, often with odd curios from the past, but somehow the effect is always harmonious and pleasing. All the rooms are unusually well stocked with books ranging from 1930s hardcover mysteries, anthologies and back issues of the *National Geographic* to recent novels and nonfiction. A decanter of cream sherry in each room provides a hospitable touch.

Service at Vagabond House is informal but gracious and attentive. In the morning, guests open their doors to the day's *San Francisco Chronicle,* and walk through the garden to the reception room to pick up their Continental breakfasts. Eating in the patio is popular, but many guests prefer to take their breakfasts back to their rooms on a tray. No other meals are served, but Carmel abounds in a wide variety of fine eating places.

VAGABOND HOUSE INN, 4th and Delores, P.O. Box 2747, Carmel-by-the-Sea, Cal. 93921; (408) 624-0988; Dennis Levett and Jewell Brown, Innkeepers. An 11-room inn in an oceanside resort town. Open all year. Rates range from $36 to $55 double occupancy; singles at a 10% discount including Continental breakfast. Private baths, some full kitchens. Not ideal for children. Pets on leash only. Visa and Master Charge credit cards accepted.

DIRECTIONS: Take Carmel exits off Rte. 1. Drive down Ocean Avenue to Delores, turn right. Inn is 2½ blocks up on the right.

Leisure deluxe in a lush setting

The flourishing forty-foot-high eucalyptus trees that give the Inn at Rancho Santa Fe its luxuriant, jungle-like setting are the result of a gigantic miscalculation by the Atcheson, Topeka and Santa Fe Railroad. The company wanted to ensure a constant supply of railroad ties for their rapidly expanding operations and, in 1906, planted three million hardy seedlings from Australia on part of the huge sandy tract they owned in Southern California. They found out in due course that it was impossible to cut a flat tie from the twisted trunk of the eucalyptus, so their fine idea was abandoned. They turned the unplanted acreage into a citrus farm, with a part set aside for residential development.

The first structure, built of adobe in California mission-style, was used by the railroad to accommodate prospective land buyers. In 1941, it was bought, along with twenty acres, and turned into a quiet resort where guests could enjoy a little peace in the California sunshine. Mary Pickford was a guest in the early days, and the eminent judge Harold Medina stayed here while doing a Greek translation. Over the years, twenty cottages have been built, and it is now a self-contained community where guests can enjoy leisurely seclusion amid verdant acacia, avocado, palm and, of course, eucalyptus trees.

The inn has been owned and managed by members of the Stephen W. Royce family since 1958; and the cottages, joined to the main building by walkways and gardens, are simply and comfortably furnished, Western-style. Many have sliding doors leading to their own patios, and the mission-style architecture has been retained throughout the complex. The Royce family's collections of antique ship models and Oriental treasures lend color and distinction to the main lounge, a huge room with a fireplace and a high, raftered ceiling. Two of the four charming dining areas are the book-lined Library Room and the breakfast room overlooking the swimming pool and patio with umbrellaed tables.

The inn maintains its own beach cottage at Del Mar and will gladly pack picnic lunches. There is tennis on the property, and golfing arrangements can be made at any of three nearby courses.

Dan Royce runs the inn on a very friendly and personal basis. One night a guest appeared at dinner coatless, and on the spot Dan loaned him his own. The guest didn't need the shirt off Dan's back, but he probably could have had that, too.

The cottages are named after flowers. This is Honeysuckle.

The main lounge exhibits the family's collection of models of antique sailing ships. OVERLEAF. *Left*: a private patio attached to one of the cottages. *Right*: the inn's grounds contain 20 acres of lush, tropical plants and trees—especially the eucalyptus shown here.

THE INN AT RANCHO SANTA FE, P.O. Box 869, Rancho Santa Fe, Calif. 92067; (714) 756-1131; Dan D. Royce, Innkeeper. A 75-room inn, with deluxe accommodations in private cottages with baths. Open all year. Rates $38 to $150 double or single; $6 extra for additional guest. Restaurant serves breakfast, lunch and dinner. Children welcome; $6 charge for pets. Visa, Master Charge, American Express and Diners Club credit cards accepted. Swimming pool, tennis courts, putting green, ping pong, badminton and horseshoe pitching. Private beach house for day use at Del Mar, 5 miles from inn.

DIRECTIONS: From Route I-5, exit at Solana Beach, Lomos Santa Fe. Drive east 4½ miles to inn on right.

A lush retreat for the status set

One of the cottages.

San Ysidro Ranch is located on the site of one of a series of missions and way stations Franciscan monks maintained along the California coast in the nineteenth century. The oldest adobe cottage, now kept as a museum, dates from 1826. Its tradition as a way station for weary travelers is still very much alive after more than a century and a half.

It opened as the San Ysidro Ranch in 1893 and was a success almost from the start. John Galsworthy stayed here while making the final revisions on *The Forsyte Saga*. Sinclair Lewis, Somerset Maugham and Winston Churchill all came here to work in the relaxed atmosphere. For some thirty years before his death in 1958, screen star Ronald Colman owned San Ysidro and used it as an exclusive hideaway for his friends. Bing Crosby and Jack Benny came often. Vivien Leigh and Laurence Olivier were married here, and John F. Kennedy honeymooned at the ranch after his marriage to Jacqueline Bouvier in 1953.

Situated on 540 acres in the hills above Montecito, west of Santa Barbara, the scenery includes views of the Pacific Ocean on one side and the Santa Ynez Mountains on the other. The bridle trails are so extensive that many people stable their own horses at the inn's facilities.

After Colman's death, the ranch changed hands many times; and by 1976, the once-proud estate was badly run down—the landscaping going to seed and the bridle trails choked with undergrowth. Enter Jim Lavenson, former president of the Plaza Hotel in New York City, who took up the banner and saved San Ysidro Ranch. He and his wife, Susie, who is in charge of the interior design, have spent well over $1,300,000 refurbishing the ranch.

All thirty-nine accommodations are private bungalows tucked away in the well-manicured gardens. Always in demand (and most expensive) is the Forest Cottage, which offers both modern furniture and antiques, a whirlpool bath and a large, secluded redwood deck with complete privacy.

The main house boasts one of the best restaurants in the state. Both steaks and prime ribs are cooked as expertly as the haute cuisine, and Julia Child is a frequent visitor.

Although Jim and Susie are nearing their second million dollars spent on San Ysidro Ranch, they admit the end is not in sight. Perfection is never cheap, but it's always worth it.

An alcove bedroom at Forest Cottage.

Cottages are spread throughout the grounds among impressive trees and plants. OVERLEAF: the intimately lit dining room; the back deck of Forest Cottage, and right, the oldest building, an 1825 adobe cottage preserved as a museum.

SAN YSIDRO RANCH, 900 San Ysidro Lane, Montecito, Calif. 93108; (805) 969-5046; Jim and Susie Lavenson, Innkeepers. Thirty-nine secluded cottages in beautifully tended gardens. Views of Pacific Ocean and Santa Ynez Mountains. Open all year. Rates $69 to $225 double. Highly rated restaurant serves breakfast, lunch and dinner. Children welcome; $6 nightly charge for pets. Visa, Master Charge and American Express credit cards accepted. Swimming pool, tennis courts, stables, trail rides.

DIRECTIONS: From Route 101, exit at San Ysidro Rd., drive east through Montecito Village to San Ysidro Lane.

Eclecticism the keynote in an Old West hotel

The Union Hotel looks like a nineteenth-century Western hotel. Gold-fringed red draperies curtain the archway leading to the large and rather formal dining room. The sitting room's décor includes potted plants and an elaborate mantel, and both rooms share the same florid wallpaper and red carpeting. The bar is hewn from solid African mahogany, and the guest rooms offer transoms numbered in etched glass, sleigh beds with handmade quilts and a decanter of wine on each dresser. The central upstairs hall has a huge pool table lit by skylights. The patterned floral wallpaper links the rooms and is even on a bathtub. But the Union Hotel is no ordinary nineteenth-century Western hotel. It is the somewhat eccentric extension of its vibrant and energetic owner, Dick Langdon.

In 1972, Dick, a highly successful meat wholesaler from Los Angeles, decided it was time to change his lifestyle. He considered buying some ranch property up north but instead wound up buying a hotel, built in 1880 and boarded up for the past nineteen years, in the virtual ghost town of Los Alamos. The antiquing trips for the restoration took a year. Among his unique acquisitions are a pair of 200-year-old Egyptian burial urns, a lamp used in *Gone with the Wind*, headlights from a 1914 Oldsmobile and a pair of swinging doors from a nineteenth-century New Orleans bordello.

The hotel is open all year, but only on Fridays, Saturdays and Sundays. "Three days a week is fun," Dick explains. "Beyond that, it becomes work." The first time guests come to the hotel, they can only reserve for one night, because Dick wants to be sure he likes them. All patrons may take a look at the available rooms and choose their own, on a first-come-first-served basis.

There is no menu at the hotel, and guests are served the table d'hôte. It always begins with cheese and crackers and a homemade soup. The most popular is Leather Apron soup, a hearty chicken-and-noodle combination from an old wagon-trail recipe. This is usually followed by a chicken or beef dish, silky-

A guest room off the upstairs hall.

smooth cornbread and dessert. Dinner is prix fixe for grownups, but children pay by weight—their own. Dick puts the youngsters on a huge butcher's scale, and the heavier they are, the more their parents pay.

Despite all the excitement and panache at the Union Hotel, Dick and his wife, Teri, like to keep the hotel simple and low-key.

The dominance of lush reds throughout the color scheme reflects the ebullient nature of the innkeeper. *At left,* the dining room. OVERLEAF: the traditional Western bar and an ornate corner of the lobby. The following pages show the upstairs hall that leads into the guest rooms, with the pool table as an added attraction.

UNION HOTEL, 362 Bell St., Los Alamos, Calif. 93440; (805) 344-2744; Dick and Teri Langdon, Innkeepers. A 14-room frontier hotel, faithfully restored. Private and shared baths. Open all year Fridays through Sundays. Rates $45 to $55 double, with deluxe breakfast: homemade cinnamon rolls, fresh fruit, coffee and brandy. Restaurant serves dinner only. No children or pets overnight. No credit cards accepted. Croquet, volleyball, badminton. Unexpected period delights, such as a restored 1917 White motorcar in which guest may go sightseeing in the area; a reflecting pool that doubles for swimming; a charming Victorian gazebo by day that at the press of a button converts to a jacuzzi accommodating 20 guests at night!

DIRECTIONS: From U.S. Rte. 101, take Los Alamos turnoff 14 miles north of Buellton, 17 miles south of Santa Maria.

2675 Benbow Dr., Garberville, Cal. 95440; (707) 923-2124; Mr. and Mrs. Watts, Innkeepers. A large, sumptuous inn, built in 1920s Tudor style, in the heart of California's redwood country. Of the 70 guest rooms, all but 3 on an upper floor have private baths. Open April 1 – Dec. 1. Rates, double, $24 – $42. Breakfast, a buffet lunch and a lavish dinner are served daily. In good weather, meals are served on the terrace. The Benbow is popular both as an overnight traveler's inn and as a resort where guests spend entire vacations. Despite the luxurious surroundings, dress is informal. Children over 12 welcome; $20 charge for pets. Visa and Master Charge. Beach for sunbathing, swimming in a private lake and a 9-hole golf course. Canoeing and hiking in the redwood forest are other popular activities.

DIRECTIONS: From San Francisco, follow Rte. 101 200 miles north to inn on left-hand side.

Westport # DEHAVEN VALLEY FARM

P.O. Box 128, Westport, Cal. 95488; (707) 964-2931; Rom Albrecht and Harry Cowan, Innkeepers. The Victorian farmhouse in a pastoral setting on the Mendocino coast was built in 1879, the only remaining structure of a former lumber town. The cozy parlor has a fireplace and piano, and the White Room downstairs has its own bath. The other 5 color-keyed guest rooms upstairs share a bath, and some have ocean views. The Dehaven Suite has a half-bath and a lovely view of the countryside, and the 2 efficiency cottages have their own baths. Gourmet meals are served family-style in the dining room, which overlooks Dehaven Creek. Continental breakfast is included in the rates, which are $35; the suite $50; the cottages $200 per week. Children not encouraged. No pets. Open all year; weekends only in winter.

DIRECTIONS: Take Rte. 1 along the coast to Westport. Two miles north of town, turn east on Branscomb Rd.

Inverness # INVERNESS LODGE

P.O. Box 126, Inverness, Cal. 94937; (415) 669-1034; Milan and Judith Prokupek, Innkeepers. A turn-of-the-century brown-shingled house in a grove of oak and acacia, with 4 guest rooms, 2 with sun decks and 1 with fireplace. Five additional rooms in a separate cottage. Dining room overlooks the garden, and Czech specialties, and pastries served from a laden dessert cart, are expertly prepared by owner-chef Milan Prokupek. Good food and peaceful surroundings are the order of the day. Children by prior arrangement. No pets. Open weekends only; usually closed in Dec. Reservations required. Rates $22.50 – $35.50 double. Restaurant open for breakfast and dinner. Visa, Master Charge and American Express.

DIRECTIONS: North on Route 1 to Point Reyes Station, just before bridge, then west and north again to Inverness Lodge.

All photographs on pages 88 to 96 by Michael Reid, except those noted.

JOSHUA GRINDLE INN

44800 Little Lake, P.O. Box 647, Mendocino, Cal. 95460; (707) 937-4143; Bill and Gwen Jacobson, Innkeepers. This white Victorian house with fine views of the village, bay and ocean was built by Joshua Grindle in 1879. Recently converted to a country inn, with 5 light and airy guest rooms. Private baths. Rates, $35–$40 double, include a full breakfast, with homemade breads and jellies. Some of the rooms have ocean views; 2 have fireplaces. The Jacobsons' collection of antiques is found throughout the house, and the original woodwork in the parlor, with piano and fireplace, can also be seen in the hall. No restaurant. Children limited. No pets. Eight weeks advance notice for weekends. Open all year. No credit cards.

DIRECTIONS: Take Rte. 1 to Mendocino, turn west on Little Lake.

Mendocino

MENDOCINO VILLAGE INN

Main Street, Box 626, Mendocino, Cal. 95460; (707) 937-0246; Robert and Beverly Sallinen, Innkeepers. Built in 1882 by a doctor, this white, Victorian house became known as the House of Doctors, since it was subsequently owned by three more. Uniquely recalling the late 19th century, it is now an inn with 13 guest rooms, 5 with private baths, including one with a parlor. Seven rooms have fireplaces, and some have ocean views. No restaurant, but a listing of those in town is available. Coffee is served. Children welcome; a $4 charge for rollaway beds. Pets by prior arrangement. Rooms with baths, $26–$32; suite, $32; room with half-bath, $29; others $16–$27. All double beds. Reservations required 1 month ahead if room preference is indicated. No credit cards.

DIRECTIONS: North on Rte. 1 to first Mendocino exit, then to Main Street.

Jenner

TIMBER COVE INN

North Coast Hwy., Jenner, Cal. 95450; (707) 847-3231; Richard Clements, Innkeeper. Massive but modern open redwood beam construction offers panoramic views of the northern Sonoma coast from most of the inn's rooms. Echoing the feeling of the rugged land and seascapes is a partially enclosed fieldstone meditating pool just off the high-timbered lobby with walk-in fireplace. Peace and beauty are the essence of Timber Cove. The restaurant will provide gourmet box lunches, with chilled wine, for guests planning to explore the area. Rates for the 45 guest rooms are $42–$68.25. All have showers or baths. About half have fireplaces; some have views of the ocean and rocky coast. Twin, double, queen- and king-sized beds available, plus one water bed. Children limited. Pets welcome. Open all year, except Dec. 24–25. Reserve well in advance for weekends. No credit cards.

DIRECTIONS: Three miles north of Fort Ross, off Rte. 1.

225 St. Helena Hwy., St. Helena, Cal. 94574; (707) 963-4423;
Jack, Essie and Steve Doty, Innkeepers. The spacious old Victorian
home was built in 1884 in this small town in the Napa Valley wine
country. The Dotys first had an antique shop here before opening
the 5 guest rooms, with shared baths, to overnight guests. Four
additional rooms, with private baths and fireplaces, in the restored
Tank House. Rates $37.50, double, in the inn, and $45–$50 in
the Tank House, including Continental breakfast, the only meal
served. Since the Dotys still run their antique business, the
charming décor is constantly changing. No children under 12; no
pets. No smoking is requested. Open all year. Reservations at least
2 weeks in advance. Visa and Master Charge.

DIRECTIONS: From Vallejo, take Rte. 29 North. Inn is just south
of the town limits of St. Helena.

HOTEL LEGER

Mokelumne Hill

Main Street, P.O. Box 50, Mokelumne Hill, Cal. 95245; (209)
286-1401; Peter Lindberg, Sue Clark, Odis Jones and Dorothy
Merritt, Innkeepers. Stone and stucco with white trim and
balconies, the hotel was originally built of wood in 1851 by George
Léger, and rebuilt after a fire in the 1860s. Always a landmark in
the Mother Lode country, the hotel has a restaurant and bar and
evokes the Gold Rush days with its frontier atmosphere. They say
the wine cellar was once a tunnel to the bordello across the street.
The attached Court House Theatre offers plays every weekend
during the summer, staged by a professional repertory group.
Weekend rates, with bath, double and single, $32; with shared
baths $24. Two Parlor Suites with baths and fireplaces, $39.
Midweek rates available on request. Children limited. No pets.
Swimming pool. Visa and Master Charge.

DIRECTIONS: From temporary I-5, take Rte. 26 east to
Mokelumne at junction of Rte. 49.

MIRAMONTE COUNTRY INN

St. Helena

1327 Railroad Avenue, St. Helena, Cal. 94574; (707) 963-3970;
Edouard Platel and Udo Nechutnys, Innkeepers. The Miramonte,
white, accented with green shutters and awning, has a fine
mountain view and has been a hostelry since it was built in 1870.
Chef de cuisine, Udo Nechutnys, runs the only French restaurant in
the area, and the dining room is reminiscent of a 19th-century
hunting lodge where dinner is served in an elegant and leisurely
way. Luncheon is on the patio, weather permitting, and in the inn's
tavern. Children welcome; pets accepted. Open all year; restaurant
closed Mondays and Tuesdays. Rates $45–$55, including Continental breakfast, and there are also 2 suites with baths, sitting
rooms and kitchenettes. Visa and Master Charge. Reservations
required.

DIRECTIONS: Rte. 29 to St. Helena, then take Hunt Ave. to
Railroad Ave.

Main St., P.O. Box 329, Murphys, Cal. 95247; (209) 728-3454; Ron Kaiser, Innkeeper. When the hotel opened in 1856, it was called "The Queen of the Sierra," and claims to be the oldest hotel in continuous operation in America. Built of limestone and stucco, it was thought to be fireproof, but a fire gutted the building in 1859. It was rebuilt more substantially and successfully survived the big fires of 1874 and 1893. The old guest book on display contains the signatures of many illustrious 19th-century visitors. The hotel has 14 guest rooms with shared baths, 1 suite, and a full-service restaurant. Rates are $20.59 double; the suite is $24.47 for 2 or $31.78 for 4. Children welcome; no pets. Visa, Master Charge and American Express. Reservations recommended, especially for summer weekends.

DIRECTIONS: From Modesto, on temporary I-5, turn east on Rte. 4 to Murphys.

RED CASTLE INN

Nevada City

Another view of the Red Castle is shown opposite.

109 Prospect, Nevada City, Cal. 95959; (916) 265-5135; Jerry Ames and Chris Dickman, Innkeepers. The colorful heyday of the Gold Rush is recalled in the décor of this 1860 red brick building, with white gingerbread trim, balconies and porches. Set on a hill overlooking this historic town, the inn's terraced gardens, with a secluded pond, offer pleasant strolls. The 2 suites, and most of the large bedrooms, have private baths, except for those on the top floor. Some guest rooms open onto balconies; the parlor has French doors leading onto the porch. The inn even has a legendary "Lady in Gray" who supposedly appears from time to time. Rates are $25–$30, including Continental breakfast. No restaurant. Small children not encouraged; pets accepted. Reservations recommended. Open all year. No credit cards.

DIRECTIONS: From I-80, take Rte. 49 to Nevada City. Take Sacramento St. to Prospect.

VINEYARD HOUSE

Coloma

Cold Spring Road, P.O. Box 176, Coloma, Cal. 95613; (916) 622-2217; Frank, Darlene and Gary Herrera, Dave Van Buskirk, Innkeepers. The white Victorian house with green trim, encircled by a porch and second-floor balcony, was built 100 years ago by Robert Chalmers as a hotel and home for his family. It was surrounded by a thriving vineyard, and Chalmers's winery prospered. He won many prizes and his wine label is framed in the front hall. The inn is furnished with Victorian antiques and the parlor has a cheerful fireplace. Dinner is served in 5 different areas, as well as on the porch in summer. The 7 guest rooms, all named after well-known Gold Rush personalities, share baths. Rates from $22, Continental breakfast included. Restaurant and bar closed Mondays and Tuesdays. No children under 16; no pets. Open all year. Reservations required. Visa.

DIRECTIONS: From U.S. Rte. 50, turn north on Rte. 49 to Coloma, and Cold Spring Rd.

P.O. Box Y, Carmel-by-the-Sea, Cal. 93921; (408) 624-3871; the McKee family, Innkeepers. This elegant and comfortable Spanish-style inn has 33 guest rooms, with private baths, phones and color TV. The McKee family is proud of its friendly and personal service. The lobby-living room has a crackling fire in cool weather; when it's warmer, the lovely garden-courtyard is a perfect place to enjoy the complimentary Continental breakfast. There is no restaurant in the inn, nor does it serve liquor, but there are many attractive restaurants and numerous bars in Carmel. Children welcome. No pets. Reservations must be made six weeks in advance. Single rooms, $25–$30; Queen, $28–$45; twin, $33–$40; King, $37–$50. American Express, Visa and Master Charge.

DIRECTIONS: One block south of Ocean Avenue, at Lincoln and Seventh, in the heart of Carmel.

GREEN GABLES

Pacific Grove

104 Fifth St., Pacific Grove, Cal. 93950; (408) 375-2095; Roger and Sally Post, Innkeepers. Despite having only 3 guest rooms, with shared baths, this inn in an 1888 mansion overlooking Monterey Bay is one of the most beautiful in a resort town that boasts many fine homes. Each guest room—Balcony Room, Garrett Room and Gable Room—is furnished with fine antiques. The inn is open only during June, July and August; prospective guests are urged to make reservations well in advance. Daily rates $32 weekdays; $35 weekends, single or double. A Continental breakfast is not included in the rate, but is the only meal offered. However, there are many excellent restaurants as well as recreational facilities in the area: golf courses, ocean beaches, pine woods and historic sites.

DIRECTIONS: From New Monterey, take Lighthouse Ave., which becomes Central Ave. in Pacific Grove. Turn right on Fifth St. Inn is last house on left.

The view of Green Gables on the opposite page, above, was photographed by George Allen.

MISSION RANCH

Carmel

26270 Dolores, Carmel-by-the-Sea, Cal. 93921; 1-800-538-8221 (408) 624-6643; Margaret Dienelt, Innkeeper. The white, two-story main house, with guest rooms, dining room and Piano Bar, is 125 years old, and was formerly a dairy. Adjacent to the Carmel Mission Basilica, second oldest in Cal., its luxuriant Monterey cypresses and eucalyptus were planted when the dairy farm was first established. The ranch overlooks the Carmel River, the bay and Point Lobos. Guest cottages have up to 3 bedrooms, phones and TV, and some have kitchenettes or fireplaces, a total of 20 units with baths. Children and pets by prior arrangement. Dinner only; dancing Friday and Saturday. Rates $26–$35 double, with $2 charge for additional person. Open all year. Tennis courts. Visa, Master Charge and American Express.

DIRECTIONS: Ten blocks south of center of Carmel, at foot of Dolores St.

Another view of the ranch is shown on the opposite page, below.

Box 250, Ocean Ave. and Monte Verde, Carmel-by-the-Sea, Cal. 93921; (408) 624-3851; Carroll M. McKee, Innkeeper. The inn's Victorian atmosphere is enhanced by period furnishings and fresh flowers. A Tiffany glass canopy found in France surmounts the door to the Red Parlor, the inn's bar, with stained-glass windows, marble-topped tables and comfortable leather armchairs. The Gazaboé, an indoor garden dining room, has a dome that opens to the sky. Full-service dining room offers meals daily, and the Fri. night seafood buffet and Sun. champagne brunch are popular. The inn has 49 rooms with baths, and the Penthouse, a luxury apartment for up to 8 people. Standard doubles $27–$34; superior doubles and twins $34–$41; queen $36–$43; king $46–$66. Children welcome. No pets. Open all year. Reservations at least 1 month ahead. Visa, Master Charge and American Express.

DIRECTIONS: West on Ocean Avenue from Rte. 1 to Monte Verde.

Big Sur

VENTANA INN

Big Sur, Cal. 93920; (408) 667-2331; Lawrence Spector, Innkeeper. Of the 6 handsome cedar buildings 1200 feet above the Pacific, all with spectacular views, 5 house guest quarters. The lobby and public rooms are in the sixth building. The 24 units include 2 duplex Townhouse Suites, each with sitting room, fireplace and wet bar downstairs; bedroom and bath upstairs. Patchwork quilts and hand-carved and painted headboards make the rooms, all with baths, distinctive. The dining room, with its own special view, is in another house, a walk or drive down the hill. Within walking distance is another restaurant, in a house originally built by Orson Welles as a wedding present for Rita Hayworth. Limited facilities for children. No pets. Rates $72–$175, double, Continental breakfast included. Jacuzzis, saunas and heated swimming pool. Visa, Master Charge, American Express.

DIRECTIONS: 2½ miles south of Big Sur State Park on Rte. 1.

Avalon

ZANE GREY PUEBLO HOTEL

P.O. Box 216, Avalon, Catalina Island, Cal. 90704; (213) 510-0966; Karen Holliday, Innkeeper. Former home of the well-loved author of popular Western novels. Designed in authentic Indian pueblo style, it is situated high on a hill commanding a superb view of town and harbor. Now a 17-guest room hotel, with private baths, it's open all year. Rates, including morning coffee and toast, Nov.–Apr. $20–$30 per person; summer $30–$60. Additional guest in room $5. No restaurant. Children welcome; no pets. Visa and Master Charge. Courtesy transportation to and from dock and airport. Swimming pool. Island tours, beaches, shops, restaurants, riding, tennis, fishing and skin diving nearby.

DIRECTIONS: From Long Beach by boat via Long Beach-Catalina Cruises or by Air Catalina.

GEORGE W. GARDNER